MW00614468

FARNSWORTH HOUSE
Ludwig Mies van der Rohe 1951

www.farnsworthhouse.org

FHBW-020

©**paulclemence**.com

published by schifferbooks.com

FARNSWORTH HOUSE
Ludwig Mies van der Rohe 1951

www.farnsworthhouse.org

FHBW-012

© **paulclemence**.com

published by schifferbooks.com

FARNSWORTH HOUSE
Ludwig Mies van der Rohe 1951
www.farnsworthhouse.org

FHBW-018

©**paulclemence**.com

published by schifferbooks.com

FARNSWORTH HOUSE
Ludwig Mies van der Rohe 1951

www.farnsworthhouse.org

©paulclemence.com

published by schifferbooks.com

FHBW-019

FARNSWORTH HOUSE

Ludwig Mies van der Rohe 1951

www.farnsworthhouse.org

© **paulclemence**.com

published by schifferbooks.com

FHBW-030

FARNSWORTH HOUSE
Ludwig Mies van der Rohe 1951

www.farnsworthhouse.org

published by schifferbooks.com

FHBW-002

FARNSWORTH HOUSE
Ludwig Mies van der Rohe 1951
www.farnsworthhouse.org

FHBW-009

©**paulclemence**.com

published by schifferbooks.com

FARNSWORTH HOUSE
Ludwig Mies van der Rohe 1951

www.farnsworthhouse.org

©**paulclemence**.com

published by schifferbooks.com

FHBW-027

FARNSWORTH HOUSE
Ludwig Mies van der Rohe 1951

www.farnsworthhouse.org

FHBW-011

©**paulclemence.**com

published by schifferbooks.com

FARNSWORTH HOUSE
Ludwig Mies van der Rohe 1951

www.farnsworthhouse.org

©**paulclemence**.com

published by schifferbooks.com

FHBW-003

FARNSWORTH HOUSE
Ludwig Mies van der Rohe 1951

www.farnsworthhouse.org

FHBW-010

©**paulclemence**.com

published by schifferbooks.com

FARNSWORTH HOUSE

Ludwig Mies van der Rohe 1951

www.farnsworthhouse.org

FHBW-022

©paulclemence.com

published by schifferbooks.com

FARNSWORTH HOUSE
Ludwig Mies van der Rohe 1951

www.farnsworthhouse.org

FHBW-007

FARNSWORTH HOUSE

Ludwig Mies van der Rohe 1951

www.farnsworthhouse.org

FHBW-006

©**paulclemence**.com

published by schifferbooks.com

FARNSWORTH HOUSE
Ludwig Mies van der Rohe 1951
www.farnsworthhouse.org

FHBW-031

©**paulclemence**.com

published by schifferbooks.com

FARNSWORTH HOUSE
Ludwig Mies van der Rohe 1951
www.farnsworthhouse.org

FARNSWORTH HOUSE
Ludwig Mies van der Rohe 1951
www.farnsworthhouse.org

FHBW-033

FARNSWORTH HOUSE
Ludwig Mies van der Rohe 1951

www.farnsworthhouse.org

FHBW-024

FARNSWORTH HOUSE
Ludwig Mies van der Rohe 1951

www.farnsworthhouse.org

FHBW-001

FARNSWORTH HOUSE
Ludwig Mies van der Rohe 1951
www.farnsworthhouse.org

FHBW-023

© **paulclemence.**com

published by schifferbooks.com